Travellers on the Narrow Road

Ellie Philpott

Open Doors

Sovereign World

Copyright © 1999 Open Doors

All rights reserved. No part of this publication may be reproduced, stored in a retrieval system, or transmitted in any form or by any means, electronic, mechanical, photocopying, recording or otherwise, without the prior written consent of the publisher.

Short extracts may be quoted for review purposes.

Scripture quotations are taken from
The Holy Bible, New International Version.
© Copyright 1983, 1978, 1984 International Bible Society.
Used by permission.

ISBN: 1 85240 251 2

SOVEREIGN WORLD LIMITED
P.O. Box 777, Tonbridge, Kent TN11 0ZS, England.

Typeset and printed in the UK by Sussex Litho Ltd, Chichester, West Sussex.

Foreword

As you read this booklet, I would like you to do one thing. Remember that these stories come from real people. Try to imagine what it must be like for them – living out a real Christian faith in a situation of incredible conflict and aggression.

After you have finished, and you still believe that there is even the faintest possibility of a human, political or military solution to the problems in this part of the Middle East – please let me know!

This could have been a six million page book. That is the number of people living in this troubled area. Six million people, each with his or her own different agenda, opinions and choices. Amongst those six million are a number of Christian men and women who are determined to share God's Word and his peace with their neighbours.

So much has been written about the 'Holy Land'. So many people have offered interpretations of prophecies. But I have a firm belief that there is only one place where the answer can be found – at the cross of Jesus Christ.

And each of us has a choice. Do we just turn a blind eye to the rapidly dwindling Church in the Middle East? Or do we get on our knees and pray? Do we support those Christians who are sacrificing so much to show those around them where real healing is to be found?

For some time, Open Doors has supported key Christians who have started real, life-changing initiatives in the Holy Land. Together we have seen some of these grow from a little seed to a great tree, bearing much fruit for God's kingdom. I am so glad you now have an opportunity to meet some of these people and hear about their work.

Brother Andrew

Introduction

As we travelled around Jerusalem and the West Bank last Christmas, the despair that filled many people's hearts was almost tangible. Not one person we met had any hope that a political solution could be really found to bring peace to this part of the Middle East. Time after time, the politicians' talks had ended in deadlock, or in empty promises.

Our goal was to speak to people who had a different story to tell. Christians from all sides, who have chosen to risk much to make their own personal stand for change in this part of the world. We discovered individuals who would not bow down to apathy and despair. Christians who firmly believe that they, with the grace of God, can make a difference in this land.

Here are their stories, for the most part told in their own words. Each one has moved outside their comfort zone. Many are commited evangelists amongst their own people. All of them have risked a great deal in order to cross the Israeli-Palestinian divide and seek to promote dialogue and understanding between the two sides. All have been profoundly changed in the process. This booklet is a tribute to them and to their extraordinary courage and faith.

Ellie Philpott

Bishara

The gentle revolutionary

"Forgiveness is the way to peace and happiness. It is also a mystery, and unless we seek it, it will remain hidden from us." Johann Christoph Arnold, *The Lost Art of Forgiving*

The journey from Jerusalem to Bethlehem certainly has its share of surprises and shocks. For a start, it's no distance at all between the two, just a matter of a 20-minute bus ride. We caught a local bus just outside the Damascus Gate, which wound its way through the Sunday morning traffic. Once outside the city, only a few scrubby hills separate the outskirts of Jerusalem from Bethlehem. But it is also home to some of the most hotly-contested land in this country, as Palestinians and Israelis clash interminably over who has right of ownership.

Bethlehem. The town where Jesus was born. Yet, today I find it very difficult to reconcile this modern-day bustle with my imagined idea of the sleepy 'little town' of the hymns. I am more concerned by the Israeli soldiers at the checkpoint into Bethlehem. Here, we are crossing from Israel into the West Bank and border controls are a necessary evil of the modern-day Holy Land.

The soldiers look so young and each is armed with a gun. I wonder what it would take to provoke them to fire. They treat their guns so casually it makes me nervous, and I wonder at how easy it is to take somebody's life.

Of course, the soldiers aren't at all interested in us. In fact, they look rather bored and wave our bus through in an unconcerned fashion. Just past the checkpoint, the road is lined with Palestinian cars, each with its distinctive blue and red number plate. These cars are not permitted to travel out of the West Bank, beyond the crossing, so their drivers traverse the checkpoint by foot and use public transport to get to their jobs in Jerusalem. At least the local buses do a roaring trade.

A bit further down the road, we yell at the driver over the noise of the engine, radio and chatter and the old bus judders to a clattering halt. We climb out, over the other bodies squashed into the cramped seats and watch him drive off in a cloud of black smoke. We turn and crunch down the gravel path into the grounds of Bethlehem Bible College, our base for the next few weeks. Nobody is in – it's Sunday and doubtless they are all still at church. We leave our cases in a doorway and wander up the road into Bethlehem to find some lunch.

The weather is unusually mild, so we find a cafe by the roadside and sit down. We are the only customers and the restaurant owner is talkative. We ask him how business is doing, and he shakes his head. "There are few tourists. It is bad. At the moment, nobody comes here."

The food is served – smoky chicken with fresh salad, hummus and olives. Afterwards we drink small cups of thick, sweet Arabic coffee flavoured with cardamom pods and laze in the warm afternoon sun. Suddenly there is a deafening blast and the cafe walls shake. I look at my colleague Sian in horror. For a moment she too is startled and then smiles. It was the sonic boom from a jet plane, high above. I relax, but not quite. Already this incident and the soldiers at the checkpoint are more than enough to remind me that I am in a conflict zone.

As we wander back down the hill to the Bible college, we smile at the children playing by the roadside. "Hello, hello!" they call out and we call back. Other people nod to us as we pass. Sian looks for an old church building she wants to show me, but we take the wrong turning and can't find it. As we scout around, we see a Palestinian family sitting outside on the patio of their house, just finishing their Sunday lunch. They call out, concerned at our disorientation.

"Can we help you? Where are you going?" We try and explain, but it's not important any more. They invite us in for coffee. We decline at first, but then agree when they press us. The head of the family is a tour guide – which explains his excellent English. We chat about his work, his family. Many of his relatives, he tells us, have left Bethlehem and gone to live abroad. "We cannot move around in this country. We are trapped here in the West Bank," he explains. "Last year, my son dropped a tourist off at the border in his car. She took a photograph of him as a memento. The next thing, he was arrested by the border guards. When he didn't return, we searched for him, and found his empty car at the border. He wasn't released until the next day. We were sick with worry."

We talked on into the afternoon. Despite our protests, fresh kebabs were cooked for us. The conversation grew humorous as we relaxed in each other's company. And, as we reluctantly rose to leave, our host looked ashamed, "I didn't ask where you are staying. Can we take you back?" We told him there was no bother, and that we were staying in the Bible College, just further down the hillside. "Aah, Bishara's place. Good man, Bishara."

Bishara's gentle face betrays the lines that pain has worn into his countenance. "The Arab-Israeli conflict had been going on even before I was born. But it took its toll in 1948, during that terrible war between Arabs and Jewish settlers. Thousands of people died – many Arabs became homeless. My own family was not spared. My father was shot dead by a stray bullet in that same year.

"There was no decent burial place for his body, as nobody dared leave the area for fear of getting shot themselves. There was no priest or minister to say a prayer. Mother was the only one who knew anything about praying, so she read from the Bible and said the Lord's Prayer. We then buried my father there in the courtyard. I was nine years old at the time – and I can still remember the details vividly."

Bishara pauses and then smiles at us. We are sitting inside the Bible College, wanting to hear his story. How he came to Bethlehem. How he has managed to accomplish so much for the sake of the Gospel in his own land. Amongst his own people.

He continued, his eyes unfocused as he gazed into the past, "In

1967, war broke out again. This affected me greatly because I was in the States at the time and I lost the right to come back home as a Palestinian citizen because of laws issued by the Israeli government. This made me so frustrated and angry.

By 1971, I had become an American citizen and was able to enter Palestine on a three month visitor's visa. During this visit I met Selwa, who was soon to become my wife. We spent the first year of our married life in the States and then returned to Bethlehem in 1972. Selwa applied for family reunion permission and I was accepted. I was once again a permanent resident of Palestine.

We were sent as missionaries to the town of Beit Jala on the outskirts of Bethlehem. We worked in a boy's school there. It was a place full of pain; the boys, all of them Palestinians, had each suffered in one way or another from the harsh treatment associated with the occupation. Hatred welled up in me and I felt powerless to help the students come to terms with their struggles, because of the anger and bitterness in my own life.

One night I cried out to God, tears pouring down my face. I asked for forgiveness for hating the Jews and for allowing that hatred to control my life. That evening, I felt God's presence in a new way. In an instant he took away the hatred, the frustration and hopelessness and transformed it into love.

After this experience, the Lord started to use me. There are so many people who are suffering, hurting and lost in this world, and God is always looking for someone to reach out to them with the Good News of Jesus Christ."

I thought of the family we had met earlier in the day. They held no hope for the future of their people. Their answer was to move away from the area and seek a better life elsewhere. A totally understandable solution, but yet, I saw in Bishara a more radical, more effective alternative.

"In 1979 God used me to start a Bible college. I had a vision for a Bible college for Palestinian Christians. Other church leaders had the same vision and asked me to go ahead. One pastor gave me 20 dollars, and God multiplied this money through a series of miraculous provisions. Even now, the college is still growing in size." Now every year, about 30 Palestinian Christian students graduate – young, enthusiastic and eager to work amongst their own people. They are encouraged to stay, for the Palestinian Church needs all the support it can get.

The statistics make depressing reading – since 1967, close to 290,000 Palestinians have left the West Bank and the Gaza Strip. Many of them are from the Christian communities. In fact, about a third of the entire Christian Palestinian population has emigrated. Bishara put it another way, "The Palestinian Christian community is slowly being squeezed out of this land by two extremist groups. Every day, secular Jews are becoming orthodox – there is a renewal within the Orthodox Jewish community; and there is certainly a real revival in Islam and an increasing interest in fundamentalism."

Then he made a comment which we were to hear again and again over the next few weeks, "My heart breaks because so many Christians around the world are not even aware that there are Palestinian Christians. We see so much focus, so much help being sent to Jewish believers – and please, please understand that is my heart too. We want to see them supported and wouldn't wish any less help for them. But I would just love for Christians in the West to understand that we are here too. We are a struggling Church – a tiny minority, and we need their prayers and love."

I was astounded by the energy and enthusiasm that we saw in this small group of Christians whilst we stayed amongst them. During the Christmas period, a number of evangelistic activities were in full swing. "We have to make the most of every opportunity," Bishara explained. "Right now, there is an openness here and we can evangelise publicly. We need wisdom, and we need sensitivity, but we can do it. And people are coming to know the Lord."

Even as we spoke, the college was full of young people. Singing and laughter floated up to Bishara's flat from the dining hall below. There, students, local Christians and workers from other Christian organisations had gathered to make up packages of Christian books and New Testaments to distribute in Bethlehem's Manger Square on Christmas Eve.

We joined in to help. The task felt endless as 10,000 packages in all were to be assembled. "On Christmas Eve, Bethlehem is filled with young Palestinians from all over the West Bank," one of the students explained. "Although nearly all of them are Muslim, they see the Christmas festivities here as carnival time and come along to join in the fun. So we use this opportunity to give them these gifts – and tell them about the real meaning of Christmas."

Bishara added, "Believe it or not, sometimes other Christians criticise us for working amongst the Muslims, but it is so important here – and we do help the local Christians enormously too. This Christmas, we are handing out food parcels to 85 of the most needy families from the Christian poor community. But, it's important to remember, the majority of Bethlehem's population is Muslim – do we ignore them? So many are needy in this area and we try to help where we can. Every year we send one or two medical teams to the refugee camps and also physical education teachers. Although we do this out of genuine concern for our fellow countrymen in need, we have found we have gained respect in the eyes of Bethlehem's Muslim community because of this. Two years ago one of the refugee camps, which has a completely Muslim population, fixed a big sign outside the front of the camp saying, 'We appreciate the work of Bethlehem Bible College'."

On Christmas Eve, we wandered down to Manger Square to see the choirs perform. I saw many young men wandering around with brightly coloured bags containing our packages. None had been thrown away. And we heard later, just one month after Christmas, that over 600 people had already returned response forms requesting more information about Jesus.

Cindy

The enemy within

"In the name of God and gods, Jerusalem has been built, fought for, destroyed and rebuilt under Canaanite, Jebusite and Israelite; under Greek, Roman and Byzantine, under Arab, Crusader, Turk and Briton. But it has been in our times that the struggle for Jerusalem has reached new peaks of passion."   Richard Z. Chesnoff,
US News and World Report August 26th 1991

Late one afternoon, we caught the local bus into Jerusalem. Inside the bus was laughter and joking – and polite curiosity. The man in front of us was quick to help me pass our fare forward to the driver. He flashed a smile. "American?" "No, English." "Aah," he nodded wisely and then resumed his conversation with his neighbour. Other faces turned away from us, having lost interest, and idly chatted.

I gazed out of the grimy window at the outskirts of Jerusalem. As we turned the corner to the Damascus Gate and the Old City, the huge rose-coloured stone blocks of the old city walls were washed by the rich winter sunlight. As in so many centuries past, traders sat outside the walls, selling fruit and vegetables spread out on gaily coloured cloths in front of them. Young children dashed around between the stalls, excited and joking.

We stepped off the bus, momentarily dazzled, assailed by the noise and sights around us. A line of palm trees, rhythmically swaying in the breeze caught my eye, when suddenly, a little boy with bright eyes ran to my side, gently tugging at my arm, "Miss, you wan' taxi?" "No thank you," I grinned and he smiled back before he shot off into the crowd.

The heavy winter sun was sinking low in the sky as we passed through the gate into the labyrinth of alleyways that is the Old City. Underfoot, the narrow stepped passageways of the Arab Quarter were uneven and the going was uncertain. We were jostled and shoved by men with carts full of goods, whilst on every side, traders called out to us, "Come, come. Look. You buy?" And in contrast to the frantic activity, old men sat at chess boards by the side of the alley, their wrinkled faces intent on the next move.

We were to meet with Cindy, a Messianic Jew, but before we did so, I wanted to see the Western Wall. Down, deeper into the bowels of the city, we wound our way. It felt as if time stood still, as if we were entering into a world centuries old. As if nothing had changed for years. Until, suddenly we were brought up short – we turned a corner and almost walked into two guards and an Israeli checkpoint, incongruous in the middle of a gloomy passageway.

As they searched through my bags and pointed me through a security scanner, I felt on edge, brought up sharply into the tension and conflict. Even as we emerged from the dark passageway into the vast white paved open space in front of the Western Wall I felt no better. Soldiers were milling about everywhere, guns slung casually over their shoulders.

The Western – or Wailing – Wall, rose high above our heads, impressive in stature. I hadn't expected it to be quite so tall, nor the space in front quite so vast. Of course this view of the wall we now had was really quite recent. Until 1967, the piazza in front of the wall housed the rambling old buildings that made up the Quarter of the Moors, but in the wake of the Six Day War, the whole area was razed to create the spacious area in which we now stood.

At the foot of the wall, the Orthodox Jews, wearing their traditional black hats and suits, stood deep in prayer, pressed against the immense blocks of stone which form their holiest site; the remnant of Herod's ancient temple compound. Just above their heads, the setting sun caught alight the globe of the Dome of the Rock. Gold flashed in our eyes. According to Muslim beliefs, this vast dome stands at the point where Mohammed rose to heaven, spoke with God, and then returned to spread the message of Islam to the world.

Beneath the dome lies the exposed rock of Mount Moriah, where Abraham was believed to have prepared to sacrifice his son. Here, so close together, are two monuments around which so much conflict has focused.

We continued on our journey, wandering up through the Jewish Quarter of the Old City on our way to Cindy's office on Jaffa Street. The pathways here too were narrow and winding, but that was where the similarity stopped. The streets of the Jewish Quarter were newly constructed and shone softly in the light which filtered from gleaming shopfronts. Inside the little boutiques, antiquities and rich fabrics caught our eyes. Gone was the chaotic bustle of the Arab Quarter, and in its place a restrained opulence.

We took one more detour which led us up through the open-air Mahaneh Yehuda market where, just a few months previously, two Palestinian suicide bombers had blown themselves up, along with 13 innocent passers-by. Another 168 people were wounded in the blast, which shocked the whole world.

"The last two bombings were very close to this office. I heard, and felt the bombs go off. They shook the whole building. We all rushed to the windows and stared out. The police station is right around the corner from us and we heard nothing but sirens for an hour or so afterwards. It was terrible. Sickening."

Cindy sighed, and leaned back in her chair, running her hands through an unruly mop of curls. We were sitting in her office in the Caspari Centre, a theological centre for Jewish and Biblical studies. Tall and slender with bright, smiling eyes, Cindy was articulate and willing to talk about life for her, a Messianic Jew living in Jerusalem.

She reflected on the recent bombing, "The only way to survive this kind of thing is to develop a thick skin and good sense of humour. We see it all here, you know. I see the soldiers on the street, everybody uptight, and I know they are going to search the rubbish for bombs to defuse again. This time it was very funny –

they picked on a bag of carrots that had been left for a nearby restaurant, and there were carrots everywhere! The funniest thing of all was a group of Japanese tourists videotaping it all. But yes, it does hit home at times. It's probably easier for me, though, because I grew up here. It's much harder for Sean, my husband, who didn't. It's difficult to get used to this country when you arrive here as an adult. On the other hand, I really believe if God calls you here, then he also gives you the resources to deal with it."

Cindy was born into a Jewish family living in the United States. Her family moved to Jerusalem when she was nine, and Cindy spent her teenage years in Israel, a self-confessed rebel. After completing her national service in the Israeli army, she travelled back to America for a visit. There she met Sean who was later to become her husband and, in her own words, "got stuck there."

The couple drifted into a nomadic hippie lifestyle, travelling around with no particular beliefs. It was while they were living in Hawaii that Sean became friendly with a group of Christians and eventually became a Christian himself. Cindy confessed to thinking him "crazy" at first. "For another thing, I was a Jew and I didn't need this Jesus," she said frankly. But gradually, as she saw a genuine change in Sean's life, Cindy realised she had something missing from her own. She too became a Christian. They were married and spent some time in California, working with students, but underneath both knew that God was calling them to Israel. For years, they put this idea on the back shelf, but God had other ideas. "Suddenly, our life just fell apart," Cindy recalled. "We got on our knees and said, 'Lord, now what do we do? This isn't working for us.' It was then that he reminded us of Israel and we knew we had to come here." Cindy is in her mid-30s and has spent part of her life away from Israel. In some ways, this means that she doesn't have the personal history that many other inhabitants of this country carry around with them. But she does have the present – and that can be difficult enough.

We turn the subject to politics, and that weary look appears on her face – the same look we have seen on the faces of so many others. "If you ask me what I think about the political situation here in Israel, I have absolutely no optimism," Cindy says with characteristic frankness. "I don't believe that is what will bring peace here. I don't trust our Israeli leaders. I don't trust Arafat. It is one big mess.

"I understand that the leaders have to try and do something, but real change in the society will only come from individuals. It has to come from enough people changing their attitude and their hearts. You can have any amount of leaders who want peace and sign agreements, but as long as there are still people killing each other, what good is that to us?"

When she arrived back in Israel, Cindy was determined to do what she could for peace in this situation. "I wanted to have a women's prayer group for Arabic and Jewish believers to meet together, but I kept waiting for someone else to do it. Finally, I was speaking to a Christian friend who lives in the West Bank and I thought, 'I need to do this. Now.' I got her to help me co-ordinate it, and we started a series of monthly prayer meetings."

Cindy feels she is in a minority. "There aren't enough Jewish believers seeking to work with Palestinian Christians," she says. "I think it stems partly from the fact that the Israelis simply aren't affected in the same way by the difficulties in this country as the Palestinians are. On the other hand, I think there is an effect on the Israelis, but it's much less visible. When an Israeli is killed, the whole country mourns. And I imagine that almost everybody in this country has lost someone; either through a bombing, or war. It is bad for both sides. And occupation itself is bad for the Israelis too, even though they are the occupiers. It is not good for an 18-year-old Israeli boy to be stuck pointing guns at a 17-year-old Palestinian boy.

"But ultimately I think fewer Israelis feel the immediate need for reconciliation. However, for the Palestinians, the need is far more pressing, because it is affecting their whole lives. I pray that God would touch Israeli hearts and cause more of us to do something for peace. It's not really that the Israeli people are ignorant of the difficulties faced by the Palestinians. I think it is just something that they choose not to look at too much. It's uncomfortable. It's 'over there'. It's not affecting me."

But Cindy is among those who have chosen to move out of

their comfort zones. She is actively involved with a Christian reconciliation organisation and helps to administrate their women's conferences. The aim is to bring women from both sides together, to overcome obstacles to peace on a personal level. But this is not easy and perhaps one of the biggest obstacles faced by everybody is fear. Both sides live with it. Not knowing when the next bomb will hit. Not knowing if someone you love will be the next victim.

"In the media, the 'other side' is so often demonised," reflects Cindy. "Both sides are guilty. Israelis learn that Arabs are terrorists and thieves. And I am sure that Palestinian children see Israeli soldiers and hear stories about some of the horrible things that happen. This cycle is self-perpetuating.

After one of the bombings in the city here, I heard some yelling in the street outside our office. I looked out and saw a group of Israeli soldiers. I think they wanted to check some Arab lad's identity card. They were shouting and dragging this boy down an alleyway. They didn't just hold his arm and walk him there, they pushed him and were really rough with him. I thought, 'Well if you didn't hate Israelis, you do now.' But I also had sympathy for the soldiers. The day before, a bomb exploded 100 metres from where they were standing, and they were uptight. I feel the same way after bombings happen. Next time you go out, you wonder if another one is going to go off. If you will be in the wrong place at the wrong time. It is very scary on a human level.

I think this underlying tension is why people here so easily go over the edge and start yelling at each other. It is not relaxing living here! A few months ago, I travelled to Cyprus for a conference. I was surprised how, the minute I got off the plane, I relaxed. Everything seemed so calm and peaceful. Sometimes you don't realise what the tension does to you until you leave the country."

It seems that life in this country exacts a penalty on every inhabitant. But the penalty for those who actively try to move towards peace seems even stronger on one level. Cindy, however, is positive, "That is true for anything where you follow God radically. You know you will have to pay something, because it's not the world's way. Impartiality isn't easy, especially when you know you're living in the world. We are affected by what we hear on the news, what we see in the street. It's so easy to just take sides. I think we constantly need to lift our eyes above the situation, and pray for God's will to be done."

But often this cost brings tremendous benefit for those who are prepared to step out. "Last year I was a small group leader at the women's reconciliation conference. There was an Israeli woman in my group who really hadn't wanted to come. She told me that God had to drag her there. But at the conference, something changed deep within her as she realised how many prejudices and fears she had been harbouring in her heart. God touched her and I was so excited to see her hugging Arab women and crying with them."

Often, people turn up with a tremendous amount of personal pain. The conferences themselves can be hard-hitting and people are encouraged not to shy away from sensitive issues. You cannot hope to move towards understanding without being real.

"I was very encouraged by the small group I was part of at the last conference," Cindy remarked. "We happened to share a lot of difficult issues that are caused by the political situation. That was good. It was so good too, to see God ministering to us and bringing a real sense of joy and healing out of our pain."

Cindy admits that the first reconciliation conference she attended was quite a learning experience for her. Everybody in the country has prejudices of some kind. But they are often very different. "People grow up with stereotypes. I know that I did, and the Lord really hit me over the head with it when I came back here. My attitude towards the Arabs in particular was bad. For me, the change came when I realised that Jesus had died for them too. I had to repent. I would say after that I changed pretty radically, but there are so many layers in each of us.

Now, I really don't have a problem with Palestinian Christians. They are my friends, and I love them. But I am not so sure about my attitude towards Palestinians who aren't Christians. It's something God has really challenged me on recently and I admit I find this a lot harder."

And we left, with Cindy's parting words lingering in our minds. "Reconciliation in this country is really in its infant stages.

But I believe that if it can spread, it will start changing things. And I see this as our mandate as Christians. This is what the Bible says, that if we Christians have real unity amongst us, the world will know we belong to God. I think this could be the greatest witness of all in this country…"

Salim

Between two worlds

> "I will never forget the chapel of the Baptist Theological Seminary in Ruschlikon, Switzerland, which had been my church for the three years. The church has four entrances. From the four sides, people come in from any side. Once they are in, they are together in one building. When you lift up your eyes you see a glass window in the chapel's ceiling. The window gives light from Heaven above, pointing to the fact that in Christ we are one since He is the light of the world."
>
> Suhail Ramadan,
> *Reconciliation Through Unification*

In many ways, we couldn't have picked a more interesting time to be travelling in the Middle East. This year three major religious festivals coincided; Christmas, Hannukah – the Jewish festival of lights, and Ramadan – the Muslim 30 days of fasting.

It was quite shocking to wander around Bethlehem on Christmas Eve and see the shops full of Christmas trees and plastic Father Christmas toys. And as I wandered down to Manger Square, where choirs sang their traditional Christmas Eve carols, I found myself surrounded by children in Father Christmas outfits ringing small handbells. The town was heaving with people. Not just tourists either, for many Muslims from West Bank villages and towns had gathered for the fun of the Christmas celebrations.

In Jerusalem, the atmosphere was festive too; children rushed to parties, cheeks flushed with excitement and the streets were filled with coloured lights, eight-branched Hannukah candlesticks and Christmas trees. Even the cold winds and rain didn't dampen peoples' enthusiasm. And to lighten the atmosphere further, there were no threats, no closures, no strikes. All was peaceful indeed –

for a while.

Gradually the excitement gave way to the more sombre days of Ramadan, when the tensions of the Muslim daily fast thickened the atmosphere; brightening after sundown when the traditional Ramadan feast meals were served, and everywhere special pancakes could be bought. In Jerusalem this year the Muslims were refused permission to use the traditional cannon, which fires at sunset every evening of Ramadan to signify the end of that day's fast. Instead, a sound grenade was used – but the effect was the same to our ears, as the booming shot rang out, echoing across the city walls.

New Year's Eve was an explosion of fireworks, colour and noise – young boys threw bangers in the streets, laughing as they stretched taut nerves a little further. But it was the festive season, and their victims always seemed to manage an indulgent smile when they discovered the cause of the disturbance.

As a result, we also had our hands full with invitations. Everybody, it seemed, was having a party, and with traditional Middle Eastern hospitality, made it sound as if our presence was vital to ensure its success. So it was with eager anticipation that we took the bus into Jerusalem on the Saturday before Christmas to visit a Hannukah party at one of the Messianic congregations in the city.

As we started off with a time of worship, I simply sat and let the beautiful music wash over me. Rich Jewish melodies filled the building, some plaintive, some forcing us to our feet, hands clapping. It was thrilling to sit with these Jewish believers, looking at the words of their songs translated on a screen, telling of Jesus the Messiah, the fulfilment of their hopes.

After the service, the games began; apple bobbing, acting out Bible stories... Our laughter and shouts rang out in a city that had seen too many tears. Then the food; small children stuffing enormous slices of cake into their tiny mouths as if this were the last chance they would ever get to eat. I glanced over and out of the corner of my eye, saw the now familiar face of Salim, absorbed in wrapping his son in tissue paper as part of some game or other.

I first met Salim the previous week, sitting in his office at the

Nashat

The young Palestinian

The advertisement in the *Al Quds* newpaper simply said:

"Verses from the Gospel:

'In the beginning was the Word, and the Word was with God, and the Word was God. He was with God in the beginning. Through him all things were made; without him nothing was made that has been made. In him was life, and that life was the light of men. The light shines in the darkness, but the darkness has not understood it.'
(Gospel according to John, 1:1-5)

We are pleased to offer you a Gospel and a magazine for free. Our address: Bible Society…"

The response was electrifying:

"Dear sir
My life is bad. I am searching for the truth. I am walking in the dark. My life is bad and full of sadness. Emptiness. There is no purpose. So I want to get rid of this life and know that life that fills the soul with peace and love. That's why I want to speak and write with you. Please send me books, videos and the New Testament." – *Response from a Muslim living in Hebron*

"Many thanks. When you sent me the Holy Bible, I started to read it. One of the problems – I don't understand it. So I tried to go to a church. Couldn't find one. Please, if you know a church where I can go and if you can send me information about the Bible and how to go to a church. Love and respect in the name of God the Redeemer." – *Response from a Muslim living in Gaza*

"Greetings,

I am a student at the Najah National University. When reading your ad in the *Al Quds* newspaper, I was delighted since I would love to get a copy of the New Testament. Because five years ago I asked another organisation to send me a Bible. They promised to send me one but I have not received it yet. Therefore I would like you to send it to me via my address since I am very interested in the Christian religion and love to know about this. Oh, how I wish to read the Gospels; John and Matthew... Many a time I engage in discussions. But my knowledge concerning this religion is nil. I would like to study it personally.

Note: I need those books in Arabic or with some translations or with a complete explanation that would fill my heart and quench my thirst.

Accept me as a friend to you...Thank you...see you."
– *Response from Jenin*

The office was hot and stuffy. We had been walking around all day, and my eyes felt heavy, but I was stirred by the words Nashat was saying. "If a door is open, you have to go inside. If not, it will close. We must work now, while it is open. Soon – who knows? I think it will be like Egypt here in five years' time. Much harder. I can see it happening. There are changes – things are tightening up. Ten years ago in Bethlehem University, there were perhaps 25 Hamas members amongst the students. Now it's one of the largest groups in the university. People are frustrated in this country. For many Muslims this is working out in a move towards fundamentalism.

But look at the responses we are getting to our advertisements. There is also a growing hunger for God in this country. Three times a week we place an advertisement in *Al Quds*, the largest Arabic newspaper in the country. We are being overwhelmed by the responses – in fact we can hardly keep up with them. It is a

Bible college in Bethlehem. But I had heard about him some time before and had been eager to meet him. To me, Salim sounded something of an enigma; a man who had grown up in two different cultures and who had learned to use this in a powerful way for peace. It was Salim who had founded the Christian reconciliation organisation, Musalaha. Salim, who was well-known in the city for his dedication to the cause of bringing Jewish and Palestinian believers together.

Another colleague of mine had met him two months earlier, and warned me, "You would think somebody dedicated to the cause of reconciliation would somehow be quiet, contemplative. Don't expect that with Salim!" And of course, it made sense. Reconciliation in this part of the world is a tough business. You have to be willing to confront, to challenge, to cope with rejection after rejection – even from your own people.

Even so, I was taken by surprise when this grinning, energetic Palestinian entered the room where we were eating. He strode into the dining hall, and was immediately laughing, joking and teasing. Talking, talking. Always, drawing people into the thread of the conversation. Now laughing, now terribly serious.

Forty-three-year-old Salim looks perhaps younger than his years, but he also carries a sense of having learned and experienced things beyond his age. "I was born in the town of Lod, near Tel Aviv. My identity is very complex and has profoundly influenced my whole life. My family are Palestinian Arabs, but we have Israeli citizenship, which gives us more privileges than many of the Palestinians who live in the West Bank and Gaza. Perhaps the most obvious being I can travel freely about this country – something many can't do."

Although Salim's religious heritage was Greek Orthodox, he attended a Jewish secondary school. There, everything Arab was considered negative. And the Jewish view of Jesus was very different to the understanding that he had grown up with.

If Salim's background is complex, his conversion to Christianity is in itself fascinating. "I became a Christian through a Bible study group of Jewish and Arab students. Then I found myself, as a Palestinian, helping to plant Messianic Jewish congregations! In some ways, my faith at that time drew very much from a Messianic context. I had never really been exposed to many Palestinian Christians."

When Salim returned from the United States, where he studied at Fuller Theological Seminary, this changed dramatically. He found himself working with both Palestinian and Jewish believers. "I had a part-time job teaching at Bethlehem Bible College and for the first time was exposed to the situation of Palestinian Christians. I taught in Arabic and found myself facing the challenge of having to 'invent' theological words in this language. There, in the town where Jesus was born, I saw some of the injustices that were happening.

"I also had another job, directing a Hebrew training programme in Jaffa, teaching young Messianic believers leadership training. I tried to convey something of what I saw in Bethlehem to my Jewish brothers and sisters in Christ, but many didn't want to hear. They were wrapped up in their own identity crisis after accepting Jesus as the Messiah."

The dual nature of Salim's working life proved a great shock to him. "I suddenly realised that there was this tremendous gap in understanding between the two groups of believers. Here I was, teaching Palestinian believers in Bethlehem and Jewish believers in Jaffa. Both groups knew Jesus as their Saviour, but were living in two completely different worlds. And most of them had never even met a believer from the other 'side'."

And so, Musalaha was born. The organisation, which takes its name from the Arabic word meaning 'reconciliation' came into being in 1989, during one of the most turbulent periods of recent Middle East history, the Intifada or Palestinian uprising.

Salim's vision was simple; to bring Jewish and Palestinian believers face to face, so that they could talk to one another. "There were so many injustices taking place and so much theological speculation, I came to the conclusion that the best theology to deal with this was reconciliation. More than anything, believers from both sides needed to talk. So much propaganda, so much dehumanisation was going on. They needed to see what they had in common, not what separated them."

It sounds easy enough, but the sheer difficulties of bringing these two groups together required tremendous determination and commitment. In the first place, the believers had to want to meet. Salim explained, "To reconcile in this situation is very hard, and people come with a lot of emotional baggage. When I confronted the students in Bethlehem with this issue, they wanted practical, real answers; 'Yes, but when I go home tonight, I will be stopped at the checkpoints and the soldiers may harass me. What do I do?' Or another asked, 'In my village, if I don't throw stones at the Israeli soldiers, I am considered a traitor. I am being humiliated every day and I feel angry, just like they do'."

The practical problems in themselves were and still are daunting. "It is often very difficult for the two groups to get permission to cross borders to meet with each other. Sometimes I feel like I spend all my time on this when we organise conferences. And then at times it all falls through and we have to cancel the whole schedule. This happened last year, after we had spent a great amount of time and money planning a conference with Jordanian Christians. At the last minute, they were refused entry visas to Israel."

When the two sides finally meet, even the language difference seems to work against them. Salim explained the effort of keeping the conference in Hebrew and Arabic. Normally people would have a tendency to revert to English – the common language – but he is aware of the importance of getting them used to hearing the other person's language. "When there is hostility between two peoples, they don't even like listening to the enemy's language – so hearing it spoken and sung is an important part of what we do. To help this, we have produced phonetic songbooks so the two sides can sing each other's songs together."

So does it work? The difficulties seemed almost insurmountable, and I was curious to see what kind of impact an organisation like Musalaha could really make. "Let me tell you some of the things we achieved this year," said Salim, his eyes bright with enthusiasm. "This is what makes it all worthwhile."

In April, we took a group of young believers on a camel trip into the Sinai desert. The Israelis had all completed their military service and the Palestinians had all grown up during the Intifada, so already they both had a background of conflict and hostility.

The desert is an ideal place for this kind of encounter as it is a place where a lot of dehumanisation and stereotypes are broken down. We got the group to do activities such as rock climbing together, so that they were even learning to trust someone from the other side with their life. In this way, the boundaries are broken down – and real friendships formed. Over the campfire in the evenings, we would gently tackle the difficult issues and allow space for people to talk and express their feelings in a location that was entirely neutral to both groups.

Everyone who came was carrying so much pain and hurt. Some more than others. We had a young Palestinian whose father had been killed by Israeli soldiers. On the other hand, the Jewish believers had also been affected by the conflict."

The trip was a tremendous success and was followed up by a powerful encounter between the same group of people, which proved an enormous challenge for the Jewish believers. The group travelled to a village in the West Bank, near the town of Ramallah. The village was hidden in the mountains, without telephones or running water. The task set the young people was to help provide an effective solution to the village's waste problem.

Because the village could not afford an efficient waste collection service, people had been dumping rubbish in the local stream, which also provided drinking water for the community. As a result, the water had become contaminated. The young people brought metal waste containers to ease the problem and installed them in place, tidying up the rubbish as they did so. They also helped two of the poorer families in the village to renovate their homes.

"I was so pleased to see what happened," commented Salim. "It was a tremendous witness to the villagers to have a group of Jews and Palestinians working side by side in their village. And I was very impressed by the courage of the Jewish believers. It was not an easy thing for them to go and spend the night in an Arab village. They risked negative reactions from their friends and families. But it meant a lot to them, to show unity with their new Palestinian friends."

Salim is quick to point out that his work has setbacks as well as encouragements and initially it took a while to get off the ground. It took time to locate believers willing to take these kind of risks.

And time to allow relationships to develop between both groups. "You simply cannot rush something like this, when so much has to be worked through on a deep personal level with every tiny step" he explained. "But now, after years of hard work, the fruit is showing."

"Let me tell you what else has happened," Salim rushed on, his words almost tripping over themselves in his enthusiasm. "We use a Jewish tour operator to organise our trips into the desert. He has helped us to plan them now for a number of years. He is not a believer himself, but I made sure he knew exactly who we were and what we were doing.

Recently I received a telephone call from him and he said, 'Salim, I want to share something with you. The government has given permission for a tour guide programme to travel and study around the Dead Sea; they want 25 Palestinians, 25 Israelis and 25 Jordanians. Where can I find these tour guides? I need people who can work together like this. I know your 'programme' works – can you find me people who have done this already?'

So you see, it is filtering through our society." Salim said. "We have been patient, and worked with small groups. Now we see that it is starting to have an influence on a wider section of our society too. That is our goal and our prayer."

Josef

Child of the Holocaust

"To this day I am shaken when I see a child, for behind him I glimpse other children. Starving, terrified, drained, they march without a backward glance toward truth and death – which are perhaps the same. Uncomplaining, unprotesting, asking no one's pity, it is as if they have had enough of living on a planet so cruel, so vile and so filled with hate that their very innocence has brought their death." Elie Wiesel, *All Rivers Run to the Sea*

Josef sat in an easy chair opposite us, his grey hair and beard adding to the sense of peace and wisdom that he introduced to the room. At times he spoke slowly, as if measuring the import of every word. But his words were full of the wisdom that has come from one who has suffered tremendously and yet found peace.

His story started in the Holocaust in Nazi Germany. I asked him if, on this trip to Israel, he had visited Yad Vashem, the Holocaust museum in Jerusalem. "No. I am an emotional person. I can never go back there, because I can't face it. On one occasion I managed to go with a friend – but…it's too much for me. It's not just what I experienced personally, it's because I also feel the hurt of humanity…"

I hadn't wanted to visit Yad Vashem either, as the thought of such death and cruelty appalled me, but I knew I had to go. So we arranged to hire a taxi to take us to the museum, which is located high on one of the many hills at the edge of Jerusalem, and hosts a collection of exhibitions, statues and memorials to the victims of the Holocaust.

My first stop was the museum building itself, which houses a step-by-step documentation of the various stages of the

Holocaust. Newspaper cuttings, commentaries and memorabilia tell the grim story. And photographs; bleak black and white shots of death camps and bodies emaciated beyond belief; of young children, grinning at a camera that was to record their last ever smile on this earth.

As I went around the museum, I noted down the different stages of persecution that happened to the Jews. I was fascinated to trace elements common to many kinds of oppression around the world; from employment restrictions, confiscation of property, limitation of personal rights and freedoms to humiliation, gross cruelty and imprisonment. All designed to dehumanise. Perhaps because then it is easier to kill.

For me, there are two places that will always stay in my memory; firstly, one of the cattle trucks that was used to take Jews to the death camps, which now stands on an old rusting piece of railway, jutting out from the hillside above the valley. I stood and gazed at this simple old-fashioned wooden brown truck where so many people had suffocated or starved to death even before they ever reached their intended destination.

The second, a small building, houses a hall of mirrors, infinitely reflecting five burning candles. Standing inside, you are surrounded by thousands of tiny, flickering flames, as a toneless voice recites the names of some of the million children who died in the Holocaust. The effect is at once disorientating and incredibly powerful.

Outside again, I wandered along a tree-lined path – the Avenue of the Righteous – dedicated to those who had helped the cause of the Jews throughout the war years. I managed, with help, to find the tree dedicated to Dutch Christian, Corrie ten Boom, where I spent some time sitting and thinking. The survivor of a Nazi concentration camp, Corrie had seen her beloved sister Betsie die there, and yet she had been able to forgive her oppressors. How could she have ever achieved that? Only by the grace of God.

Josef's voice snatched me away from my memories of that visit as he began to tell his own story. At times, he stopped, brought up short by recollections that were too painful, but as he spoke, jumping backwards and forwards from the past to the present, we were able to piece together a picture of his life:

"I was born in Frankfurt back in 1929. My parents were Eastern European Jews, who had emigrated to Germany from Poland to escape the persecution and poverty there. They thought they had found a place where they could be happy and where we could live in peace as a family, but they soon discovered they were so wrong.

When I was only three years old, I remember looking out of our window, down onto the Ostendstrasse. As I gazed onto the street, a group of young men in uniform marched past our house, singing a song. The words drifted up to us on the breeze and even now in my mind's eye, I can see the horror on my parents' faces as they realised what the men were singing, 'Wenn Judenblut vom Messer spritzt' – when Jewish blood runs from our knives...

As a child, I picked up the tension in the atmosphere. My parents were terrified and had no idea of what the future would hold for us. Hushed conversations in strained voices made me still more nervous. Then came the day when we moved again. In late 1933, we returned to the town of Rozwadow in Poland. A town full of Jewish people – tailors, craftsmen, merchants and many others.

But there was to be no peace for us here either. In 1939 war broke out, and within a matter of weeks, the Germans had invaded our town. My father and older brother hid for as long as they could, until the day when we were all ordered to collect our belongings and congregate in the town square.

We were marched along to the San River, our belongings tied up in little bundles on our backs. My parents had hidden their savings in my little sister's clothing, hoping nobody would think to search her. Sure enough, the soldiers searched us as soon as we came to the river, and everything of value was stripped off us – except for the money my sister carried, which they never found.

On the other side of the river, we were left to our own devices. We wandered along until we came to a little village, where we took shelter for a while. But after a couple of days, the rumours started – 'The Germans are coming! They're going to occupy the village!' So we moved on again, carrying what few belongings remained to us.

We hoped to reach the Russian border, and with it, safety; but as dusk fell, we were attacked by a group of thugs demanding our valuables. We didn't dare resist, and gave over what little we had left. Thankfully, they then left us alone.

Finally, we made it to Siberia, where we spent the next few years, but they were sad ones for us. My mother died of typhoid and gradually the family was broken up. By the age of 14 I found myself completely alone in the world. I escaped to Palestine, hoping to make a new life for myself there. The year was 1943.

Gradually, the trickle of immigrants into my new homeland became a river and then a mighty tide. Stories of atrocities were exchanged between survivors of the dreadful Holocaust. Stories that made my heart feel like stone. The 'old men' telling these tales were only young boys of 13 and 14 but already they had lived a lifetime and more...

I was filled with anger and bitterness which was only fuelled by the behaviour of the British administration. How dare they restrict the immigration of Holocaust survivors! How could they show so little sympathy? How could they ever begin to imagine what we had been through?

When the British left in 1948, the fighting began in earnest. I was 19 and desperate for action. We Jews were determined never, never to let these things happen to us again – no matter what the cost. I told myself I was not going to be a victim any more.

I joined an elite corps of the army. I didn't even care what happened to me – I had no family to worry about me.

One day, my unit was stationed at a village called Lod – the Lydda of the Bible. The villagers had been ordered to leave by the Israeli army, but to my colleagues' minds, they weren't leaving fast enough. Our orders were not to brutalise them, but many of my fellow soldiers just saw red. We had been ordered to search the Palestinians for valuables – and some did so using despicable methods, beating and interrogating them brutally. Some of the Palestinians even died as a result.

I was horrified at the behaviour I saw. I hated the Germans for what they had done to me, but had no particular feelings against the Palestinians. As I looked on, I saw the fear in the eyes of the young Palestinian children we had been ordered to search. Suddenly my childhood flashed before my eyes. Images of myself being brutally searched by soldiers came unbidden to my mind. I too had been forced out of my home and everything of value taken from me.

I could hardly continue. I felt overwhelmed by guilt at being part of an army that was hurting the Palestinians in the same way we had been hurt. Wordlessly I carried out my orders, but the anger inside me had died. And in its place, was a tiny seed – the beginning of peace.

I left the army as soon as I could and wandered for years, an exile – fleeing from the demons inside me, trying to find some way to reconcile my experiences and all that had happened to me. Trying to expunge the inner turmoil of hatred, bitterness, anger and guilt.

My journey to God was a long one and even when I found him, it took many years to know true release. The path towards forgiveness and healing is not an easy one. I still shudder to think of the incredible evil that exists in our world.

But now I believe I have found real peace. The peace that only Jesus can bring. I know where I am going to. And I know what I have given my life to – my God.

I am now 69 years old. I thought I had finished my journeying in the way of peace, but God has brought me back to Israel, where you see me now. Through a series of circumstances, I have been able to contact a Palestinian Christian – a man who was living in the town of Lod when we ransacked it as soldiers, so many years ago. I have come here to pray with him – to ask his forgiveness – even though I know I have God's forgiveness. For me, this act is important.

I want to do what I can to bring about peace in this country. I see it as a kind of national conflict. In the Palestinian's eyes, the Jews are foreigners here. We came into their land – it's been theirs for centuries and now we turn up and claim it as our own. But for us Jews, this is the land we have dreamed of, prayed for – from my childhood I knew about it. We prayed every day 'Bring us back to the land.'

So we have this conflict – from two different claims and the result is – fighting! This is how I think today. It is not important for me who is right and who is not right. But people are still suffering here; men, women and especially children. So I have decided to seek a different way. To seek how people can live together in harmony.

We are commanded in the Bible to seek the Kingdom of God. It was one of Jesus' main concerns. He speaks about it in many instances; how the world will only recognise that he has come from the Father when they see unity amongst us. That is my concern now. Not just that we should have our own salvation, but we should express God's heart in unity amongst us.

When I see unforgiveness, I believe this is Satan's work. He is the one who always wants to separate men from men. Jesus came to bring us together. Satan succeeds sometimes, because of this sinful side in each of us which listens to his voice and says forgiveness is impossible. But I know forgiveness is possible – I have experienced it myself. And I have learned to forgive."

full time job. George here is hard pressed. And look where they are coming from – Gaza, Hebron, Nablus – from places where there is hardly any Christian witness at all!"

We were sitting in the office of the Bible Society in Jerusalem. Nashat, a young Palestinian in his 20s has been working with the Society for some years. The sheer energy and enthusiasm he and his friends throw into their work and their personal witness is leading to some very exciting progress indeed.

"Last Easter a group of us organised a huge open air concert in the square right in the heart of the Christian Quarter. It wasn't easy even to get it off the ground. So few churches in Jerusalem are happy to work together. There is so much disunity and arguing, it breaks my heart. But this time, praise God, we managed it and invited leaders from several different denominations to speak. We also asked an ex-drug addict we have been working with to give his testimony. He was happy to do so, but none of us anticipated the result. It was as if revival broke out that day in the Old City.

There is a terrible drug problem in the Christian Quarter of the Old City. Some say over 80 per cent of the people who live there are involved in some way. Many young people start taking drugs when they are 14 or 15. They take marijuana, hash, crack and a new drug called 'trip'. It's very difficult for them to avoid the drug scene here, particularly as all the dealers are based in the Christian Quarter too.

Michael, who spoke at our meeting, had a very sad story. He was well-known in the quarter as a hopeless case. All he cared about was getting his next fix. His wife had kicked him out of their home and he was living with his parents. Well, Michael was invited to a meeting at my friend's house. God touched him powerfully, and he broke down in tears. The next day, he was invited to church, and there he gave his life to God. The change in him was dramatic. He really was a new man.

When he spoke at the open air meeting, the atmosphere was amazing. The people were really moved because they knew he was in such a desperate state. Some people in the crowd were crying. And then it was as if revival had come. God touched many at the meeting and several drug addicts were healed. They wanted to go to church too. Others wanted to know why and how Michael had changed.

We spent a lot of time trying to help the ex-addicts continue in their new life. Sadly, we have seen some frustrations, and a number of them have fallen away, but there are still those who are continuing in the faith. And others who want to know more."

Nashat has also spent time organising a series of evangelistic concerts, again aimed at a Palestinian audience. A Lebanese Christian singer called Lydia has just completed a tour of Israel and as a result of her witness, many Palestinians have become Christians. One story Nashat told us was particularly interesting:

"Recently we went with Lydia to Bethlehem University and met with a small group of about seven Christian students, just to encourage them. The area is largely Muslim and it was good for them to be involved in outreach amongst their people. As we just prayed together and sang Christian songs, there was a knock on the door and three students walked into the room, surprised to find us there.

They told us they were supposed to have a lecture in that room, but no-one else had turned up. Anyway, we invited them in and told them we were doing a Bible study. Lydia played some songs for us on the guitar and started talking to one of the students, a Muslim.

He was really interested in what she had to say, and spent nearly an hour with us, asking so many questions. We invited him to a youth meeting we were holding in the area, and he came along. There my colleague gave his testimony – he'd had quite a rebellious childhood before he became a Christian! Then Lydia sang there too.

The Muslim lad was really touched by the talk, and came up to speak to Lydia afterwards. 'God didn't bring you here for nothing.' He told her. 'I didn't come to that classroom for nothing. I have never been to that room in my life before. I came with my friends, only because they had invited me to come along to their lecture with them. It turned out there was a strike that day and no lectures were held. But instead, I received Jesus as my Lord! I will stop celebrating my birthday and start celebrating it on 20th November!'

It turned out that the young Muslim too was a singer and had been impressed by the quality of Lydia's voice. He was intrigued to know why she only sang Christian songs and gave these concerts when she could have been a big success commercially. Lydia explained how God provided her with everything she needed and that commercial success didn't appeal to her. It was that which challenged him profoundly…"

But Nashat isn't just concerned to work for God amongst his own Palestinian people. He has a real longing to see the Jews come to know Christ, and has made an incredible commitment to cross the barriers in order to work with them.

"I followed a study course at the Jewish Institute. This was a deliberate choice because I wanted to really get to know Jewish people. I had been attending a Messianic Jewish congregation for some time, so this was a further step for me.

I was the only Arab there, and at first my fellow students were very suspicious of me. As they gradually got to know me as a person, they began to see me as Nashat and not just another Arab. I prayed for my fellow students every day and asked God for opportunities to witness to them. Whenever I had the chance, I would do practical things for them, to show God's love. I had a car, and was happy to give them lifts to places. When they saw the cross in my car, they would ask me questions, and often I was able to give them a copy of the New Testament. They wanted to know why my life was so different from theirs!

Once, I really had a chance to show them the power of God. We had a very difficult examination coming up – one which many of the students on my course failed, year after year. Some of my classmates had devised a plan to cheat in this exam and they wanted me to join in with them. They were really surprised when I refused, and I sat at the front of the hall, so I wouldn't be involved.

After the exam had finished, they all came over to me and said I was bound to fail. I must admit the questions were terribly difficult, and when they told me what a fool I was for not joining in with them, I have to say I felt awful. I was very depressed and was sure I would fail the exam. I even questioned my own actions and wondered if I should have cheated after all.

Three weeks later, I had a phone call from one of the other students. She was really excited, telling me that she'd just heard she'd passed the exam. After we finished talking, I rang the college to find out how I had done. My heart was heavy, but to my amazement I discovered that I had passed too!

I called my friend back to tell her my good news – she was so stunned she could hardly speak. She found it hard to believe I'd passed, especially as so many others had failed the exam this year too, including quite a few of those who'd cheated. She asked me how I'd managed to pass the exam, and I explained that I believed God had helped me and he'd honoured my integrity. As a result she now invites me round to see her family – she has a husband and three children, and she asks me to share my beliefs with them. Because of my time at the college, I was able not just to speak to the others, but to witness to them through my life too."

I wondered how Nashat was able to reconcile his witness to the Jewish people with his position in their country. Sometimes during the course of his work, he meets with many frustrations because of the security restrictions hindering travel in the country. But Nashat's solution is a positive one;

"I love to share about Jesus with the Israeli soldiers at the checkpoints, and I always carry Hebrew New Testaments in my car so that I can give them one, if they are interested. That makes me feel like I have achieved something good in this situation. If they are aggressive, maybe I am able to show them something of Christ's love in return."

It sounded good, but I wanted to find out really how difficult this kind of attitude was. It must be so hard to maintain the right attitude in situations where you are an innocent victim. Nashat enlightened us, "Yes, of course there are times when I get frustrated and angry. Especially when I have travelled down to Gaza, where the situation is especially difficult for my people. But I try not to feel negative. I love the Jewish people, and I believe that many of them will come to the Lord through Palestinian Christians. They will see we are different by our love for them."

Avichai

Into the melting pot

"We shall draw nearer to God, not by trying to avoid the sufferings inherent in all loves, but by accepting them and offering them to Him; throwing away all defensive armour."
C.S. Lewis, *The Four Loves*

I was in the kitchen, frantically stirring a sauce that wouldn't thicken. It was Christmas Eve and 14 hungry guests sat next door in the annexe, sprawled around a long table decorated with fruit and flowers. It felt as if we'd spent the whole day cooking, but I knew that wasn't true really. Suddenly, the sound of singing broke through into the clatter of pans.

In the superb acoustics of the high-ceilinged annexe, the voices of our guests rose in a beautiful harmony. The words suddenly reminded me what this evening meant to all of us;

*"Silent night, holy night
All is calm all is bright..."*

My panic left me.

I took breath later and looked at my companions around the table. An oddly-assorted group of friends who we invited to spend Christmas Eve with us. All were travellers here, some passing through briefly, others staying longer. And each with their own particular reason for being in this place at this time; Carole, an American lawyer who had spent time teaching English in the Middle East and was now travelling with a friend; Sue, a journalist taking a few days off a hectic schedule to visit family; Maggie, an American living in Jerusalem and working with Russian Jewish immigrants; Danielle, a volunteer working on a kibbutz...

Later, we would split up for the evening; some to go and sing carols at the Shepherd's Fields, others to go down to Manger Square for the traditional Christmas celebrations there. But for now, we were enjoying the soft candlelight and hearing one another's stories.

I came back into the room as Sue was speaking. "Really, this guy impressed me so much. His honesty is incredible. And he's got real courage to do what he's doing." Avichai. The name stuck in my mind, and when I was back in England, I contacted Sue again. Could she give me more details about this young Israeli? I had wanted to meet with him myself, but sadly we ran out of time.

What came back to me was an extraordinary story in Avichai's own words:

"First a little bit about myself. I became a believer in August of 1988. Before that I was an agnostic I suppose, but I came from a traditional Jewish family. I was born in Tel Aviv. After I served my obligatory three years in the Israeli army I decided to go on a trip to Europe to see some of the works of art I had read about in my studies at college.

Just before I left, my sister became a believer. She told me what had happened to her, but I wasn't really interested. I just thought, this is for her, not me. All the same, I took the Bible she gave me on my travels. I found it actually quite interesting – here a Bible is the Old Testament. But she gave me the Old and New Testaments together in one book.

As I travelled around Europe, I got more and more convinced that this book was the Word of God. I eventually became a believer in Amsterdam at a place called The Shelter. I stayed there for a few weeks, then came back to Israel at the beginning of 1989, where I spent two years in Tel Aviv working as an evangelist. Finally, I moved to Jerusalem and spent another three years here doing the same thing.

It's important to understand what it means to a Jew here who becomes a believer. It's not an easy thing. When we become Christians, we go against everything: our culture, our society, our family. In my case, my father was very much opposed to my conversion. So we have to establish something here – an Israeli mentality, not a Western Christian mentality. At the moment, we have been very influenced by Western Church life, and many Jewish believers here want to go back to our roots. It's true to say that 2,000 years ago there was no Christianity as such – everything was Jewish. The whole faith in Jesus was very Jewish.

However, one of the down sides is that it is very easy to become absorbed in the whole business of finding your identity as a Jewish believer. I think that is a real challenge to us here. At first, when I came back to Israel, I was told to increase my knowledge of Judaism, so to become a better Jew and a better believer. Everything that surrounded me dealt with the salvation of Israel, the salvation of my Jewish friends and family. And the Arabs were just totally ignored. It was a subject I just had no interest in.

I think I first began to understand my real feelings towards the Arabs after I had met my wife. I was married in 1991. I was doing some street evangelism when she walked by and heard the Gospel. Later, she became a believer and we married. She is originally from Sweden and her parents are Jewish – Holocaust survivors. Because she grew up in Sweden, she had no negative feelings towards the Arabs. She liked them.

I remember as we became friends and decided to get married, I was looking through her stuff and one day I found this phone book and all through the phone book there were names of these Arab people. I asked her, 'What is this? What are all these Arab names doing in here?' She said, 'These are friends of mine. I go to visit them from time to time.' I was angry, saying, 'Come on, this is ridiculous, I mean, forget it. From now on, no Arab friends.'

You need to know, this is how I grew up. I'm an Israeli and I'm Jewish; and I have a culture that has injected into me for years hatred towards the Arabs. I hated Arabs – for me a good Arab was a dead Arab. But at first, I didn't even realise I thought that way. It was only things like the incident with the phone book that started to show me.

I first met Salim when he was teaching at the Bible college in Jaffa and he invited us to a Musalaha desert camp. I think the process of healing for me started from that point. I didn't even understand why I was going, because I didn't think I hated the Arabs. I thought, well, you know, some Arabs are believers, that's fine for them. But I began to realise that apathy is even comparable to hatred. When you are apathetic towards somebody, you don't really care what happens to him. When you hate somebody, you care that something bad will happen, but at least you listen to his problems, and then you want something bad to happen!

That was the beginning of a healing process in my heart. First of all, understanding that I hated the Arabs. Secondly, admitting that God was working among them as well as among the Jewish people. And the third realisation, was that to my amazement, I felt closer to Arab believers than I felt to any Jewish believer who hadn't come from Israel. The culture was so similar; the food and so on.

But even so, it was relatively easy for us to love one another in isolated situations. In the desert, nobody is watching you; you can love the Arabs, you can say you care for them, worship with them, pray with them. But when you go back to your own surroundings, then the challenge comes.

I remember being shocked at an incident that happened to me three years after my first desert trip. I was playing basketball with some friends, when a group of Arabs on the court next to us were suddenly attacked by a gang of Jewish young men. They started kicking and beating the Arabs, but I stood by watching the whole thing and I couldn't lift a finger! That really disturbed me. And I realised that this was something so deep; that God had to transform my heart and take me to a place where I wouldn't just say, 'Love thy neighbour as thyself' but really do it.

I love this example that I heard on the news about a Jewish Orthodox lady. She was in the market, trying to do her shopping, when she saw an Arab terrorist go to stab a little girl. For some reason, something interrupted him and he ran off. He was followed by an angry mob, running after him and trying to lynch him in the street. By mistake, this Arab guy tripped over just by this lady. She understood what was happening and literally laid on top of him, protecting him from the mob. By doing so, she saved his life, because they would have killed him there and then.

This story is something I hold very close to my heart – it's like a light to my path. I hope I will never be involved in a situation like this, but I do hope that in situations where I have to stand up for my Arab friends, that I am able to do so, just as Jesus stood for righteousness. I think God has taken me into some situations a bit like that. Once I had to go and bail out an Arab friend who was in prison – the only way for him to get out was for a Jew to go and sign for him.

There is a cost involved in taking this path, there's no doubt about it. Since I have stood for the rights of Arabs, I have had many strong discussions with people and even lost some friends. But in some way, this has helped my faith so much; because it brought me to a place where I knew I had to die for my friends. Many people who were good friends of mine decided that maybe I'm not such a good believer, loving the Arabs as much as I do. But what happened deep inside my heart was a true change and it has brought me closer to the Lord.

I have an Arab friend called Tanas who I met on a Musalaha trip. But that took some doing! His family didn't accept our friendship in the beginning and neither did mine. They were always saying to me, 'What? You're going to Bethlehem? Are you crazy? Nobody goes there!' But I learned that this friendship was valuable to me. And it was little things that brought us closer together: getting my car repaired in Bethlehem because it was cheaper there; he would come here to Jerusalem and go out to a restaurant because the restaurants are nicer here. But this intimacy also means sharing problems, standing for one another in times of trouble. Being there.

You must understand too how much the Holocaust has permeated our society. You know, when they came out of the concentration camps, the Jewish people lost everything. They were rich people; suddenly they were poor. They had food; suddenly they had no food. They had families; suddenly they had no-one. Many of them, afterwards would just save everything. They wouldn't throw anything away, even if it went bad!

I understand this, but it's almost 60 years since the Holocaust, and in a right sense, we have to escape it. It just destroys us.

But, too, change is not easy. The hatred comes back. It's stupid to think that we can be changed overnight. The hatred is rooted in our hearts and it takes time for things to change. The hatred can come back. It just does. You just don't realise that this is a process of healing which is important for us to go through. Because as we go through this process of healing, on both sides, we get closer to God and we realise the heart of Jesus Christ. If it was a one-minute instant thing, we wouldn't appreciate so much what Jesus had done.

I think that as we go through it, slowly, slowly, and let the truth of Jesus break down this wall that is in our hearts, we start not to care whether someone is a Jew or an Arab. We just start loving them and being closer to them and learning to pray together, and that's a beautiful thing."

The refugees

No longer my enemy

"I am convinced that the solution of this problem is not to be reached by bullets or bombs...I pray that peace may come immediately to Palestine, peace emanating from the hearts of the peoples themselves, the only true instrument by which it can be achieved, a peace built on enduring foundations..."
May 13th 1948: Farewell speech by Sir Alan Cunningham, British High Commissioner at the end of the British Mandate

"We are wounded Palestinians. Our son Mohammed died. Our children were throwing stones during the Intifada. They never had an education, because they were in and out of prison all their teenage years."

We are sitting in the Deheishah refugee camp in Bethlehem, sharing coffee with a Palestinian family. The house is spartan, but comfortable. It used to consist of one breeze block room – the one in which we're sitting. But the family have extended their 'property' and now the house has two living rooms, three bedrooms and a kitchen.

The grandfather speaks, "There are 10,000 refugees in this camp alone. We have been here since 1948. At the time this area was Jordanian, and we thought we would be safe here. At first we were given tents, but after a few years the tents weren't any good. The United Nations then built us breeze block shelters to live in – one room for my whole family. Thirteen people."

His family is courteous and welcoming. The grandfather and his wife dominate the conversation whilst their son, perhaps in his late 20s, sits and listens respectfully. A young girl lingers, almost out of sight in a back room, a newborn baby in her arms. I go to take a look at the baby, and she smiles shyly. We are treated as honoured guests.

The room is dominated by pictures of a young teenage boy. Behind the sofa, a huge pencil portrait gazes down at us, the eyes haunting and sad. The picture is surrounded by paintings and photographs of the same boy, one of them showing him in a hospital wearing some kind of surgical gown. Scattered in between these are Palestinian flags of all shapes and sizes, and a woodcarved fist, punching menacingly out of its frame.

A little boy is perched on the edge of the sofa, his cheeks bright with fever and his breath rasping. "He is called Mohammed in memory of his uncle," we are told. The family turn to the little boy and ask him something. He replies softly, and then buries his head in his father's lap, suddenly shy at the attention. Sian translates, "They asked him what happened to his uncle, and the little boy replied, 'The Jews killed him.'"

I feel overwhelmed by the sense of hopelessness. The family is not Christian, and it seemed to us, could not let go of the past. As if in some way, the pictures of this young teenage boy on their walls could keep him alive for them.

We spoke for some time, listening as they poured out years of grief: "They say outside that there is peace in this country, but there is no peace. My son was sacrificed to this cause. Another lost his eye. My other sons are all on the run because the Israelis want to shoot them.

During the Intifada, we would hide people. The soldiers would come looking for them and I would refuse to open the door. The soldiers came into the house several times; they broke the windows and beat me. We couldn't have any pictures of our son on the walls at that time; they would have firebombed the house."

"Have you ever met an Israeli on a friendly basis?" I asked, curious. "Yes," the grandmother replied. "Through the Peace Now movement. Just today we had a call from an Israeli friend. We asked her to bring us a special kind of food. She comes, and we go together to visit Mohammed's tomb. I have friends among the Jewish people."

I wondered, amidst their struggles, how this family perceived their future. "Do you have any hope?" I asked. The answer came back:"We'll have to wait and see. Without hope, we cannot exist."

❖ ❖ ❖ ❖

Two days later, I found myself on the way to Ramallah, to pay a visit to some other Palestinian refugees. In itself, the journey to Ramallah was eventful. We caught a bus into Jerusalem and interrogated taxi drivers in the bustle outside the Damascus Gate, but our budget was limited and we didn't want to pay the prices they were asking, so we scouted round for a local bus and finally tracked one down, just around the corner.

As usual, inquisitive stares followed us, but today they felt intrusive and I was fed up with being the centre of attention. I felt uncomfortable – squashed and irritable. My bag full of equipment – a tape recorder, two cameras, microphone and adapter – dug into my knees. I couldn't remember when I last changed the batteries on my tape recorder, and began to panic. The charged atmosphere in this country was beginning to get to me...

We were disgorged into the middle of Ramallah and stood there, disorientated, the object of polite curiosity. Few tourists ever visit this bustling West Bank town. We were there to meet with a group of Christian ladies who had attended a reconciliation conference. They were all members of the Baptist church in Ramallah. And so, we were invited to their Christmas service and offered the opportunity to speak with them afterwards.

After a long walk and many false turns, we finally walked around a corner and saw a modest building topped with a cross – we had made it. Outside, children ducked and dived, playing noisy games, dressed in their Sunday best, whilst the older people quietly made their way inside the building and stood, drinking coffee and talking.

We were greeted warmly by Munir, the pastor, and invited inside. He was proud of his church building, which had just been redecorated. An adapted house, the meeting room was simple with wooden benches and a raised platform at one end. As the church filled up, I noticed we were surrounded by women. There were hardly any men at the service. Perhaps they were all working – Sunday is not a day of rest in this Muslim-dominated area.

After the service, everybody spilled outside into the warm

sunshine. Again, small cups of sweet Arabic coffee were offered. I drank mine gratefully, wondering when we would get the chance to eat on our hit and miss schedules.

Munir gestured and quietly drew us back into the church. On a sofa, three ladies were seated, looking slightly suspicious of us. Two were elderly, with craggy faces and stray grey hairs escaping from pretty headscarves. They sat with handbags on their laps, arms folded politely. To their left, sat a younger woman. I guessed in her late 40s.

There were times as we spoke to people that I had a feeling we needed to 'prove' ourselves to those we met. In this divided, confused country, nobody knew where our allegiances lay. Or what we would say about them. We were two western women, wanting to pry into their lives. Why should they tell us anything? Let alone touch on the painful experiences that had profoundly affected them. And yet, I was amazed at the way in which they always chose to talk. And it seemed to me as if a pattern was emerging.

Initially we would receive polite, but friendly replies to our questioning. Non-committal, and not really telling us anything we didn't know already. But that wasn't what we were after. We wanted to find the truth – to gain an insight into what many people in this country really thought and felt. We didn't want the clinical replies.

Our answers came, but needed much patience. Often as we spoke and listened, we would notice a gradual change come over the person we were talking to. As they relaxed and got used to us, the real depth of feeling would start to emerge. And I was deeply shocked at what I heard. Horrified at the raw, burning pain in so many peoples' lives.

These women were no exception. Their initial replies skimmed the surface; "We enjoyed the women's reconciliation conference." "The food was bad." "Yes, I liked to talk to the Israeli women."

Then the replies to our questions began to rain thick and fast. The women were eager to talk, and their stories came out in fragmented bursts, interspersed with comments from the others, until my head whirled, trying to make sense of three disjointed stories, now in the past, now in the present. Suddenly, a thread seemed to jump out of the chaos, a quiet, sad, insistent voice. That of the older lady, whose kind eyes peeped out from underneath her scarf. I later discovered she was called Hanan.

"Until I die, I will never forget that day in 1948. We heard the Israeli soldiers were coming to Haifa and we were terrified. My husband told me to pack a few things and get ready to leave the area. We figured we would only be gone for a couple of weeks, so we just packed the bare essentials. I had three children at the time – one was a small baby.

We fled to Ramallah and were given a room to shelter in. There was one small mattress to sleep on. I was breastfeeding the baby and needed milk to drink but we couldn't even afford one small glass. The children were so hungry, they cried constantly. I was at my wit's end and didn't know what to do. They wouldn't sleep, because of the hunger. Then my husband had an idea. He pretended to go out and get some food, hoping the children would fall asleep while he was gone – before he came back empty handed. It worked – that time.

In Haifa we had owned a large house and a factory on Jaffa Street. We used to live like kings!" She paused, gazing into the distance as she relived the memories. "Did you ever go back?" I asked.

"Our house was demolished five years after we left. But before then, I did go back once, to visit. I had left an open Bible in one of the rooms, hoping that somebody would read it. The family living in my house let me in. I described to them what had been in each room, but they said they had never seen the furniture…"

Since then, it seemed, Hanan had made a life for herself and her family in Ramallah. First, living in utter poverty as refugees. Gradually scraping a living and building up a home. But, she told us, that wasn't the end of her problems. Simply living in the West Bank poses all kinds of restrictions for Palestinians. "Before the Intifada, we were living together like brothers and sisters; Jews and Palestinians. Now things are so different."

Hanan sighed as she gave us an example, "My sister is living in Bethlehem. She has cancer, so I try to visit her once a week. It used to take me half an hour to get there. Now, because of the checkpoints and restrictions it can take me an hour and a half.

Sometimes, if there is trouble, I am turned away, or I don't even bother to travel. By the time I get to her house, I am very tired."

She continued, "My grandchildren lived with me for a while because my daughter couldn't take care of them. Once, eight Israeli soldiers came into my house at three in the morning. They started searching the house, turning everything upside down. It terrorised the children. This kind of thing has such a bad impact on them. I have sent them all to the United States, for their safety – but I miss them so much, and now I wish they were here with me."

The other older lady listened intently to Hanan's words, nodding every now and then. After a while, she leaned forward on the couch and put her hand gently on my knee. Then she said softly, "People here are eating, drinking and sleeping, but their souls are crushed. They are dead."

I felt overwhelmed in the presence of so much distress, and yet what struck me more forcibly was the attitude of these ladies, particularly compared with the refugee family we met in Bethlehem. Here was deep sadness, and a sense of frustration, but no bitterness. No recrimination. No blame.

I hardly dared move the conversation on to the women's conference, but I was fascinated to know what had happened to Hanan there. Why had she gone? Had she managed to confront her past in the presence of those she could be forgiven for thinking of as the enemy?

Why did she want to go? Hanan's voice was positive, "We all wanted to express our worries for our families. It was so good to do that. We were drinking coffee, eating together with Israeli believers – and we felt as one. I didn't find it difficult. I didn't even notice that they were Israeli. We cried together and wished for peace. I saw the same concerns for their families in them. We want real peace. Maybe by meeting like this, we can do something. I don't know."

At Hanan's side, Selwa, the younger woman, suddenly spoke up. "I was nervous to go. Before the conference, I was too afraid to visit an Israeli woman in her house. All my neighbours said I was crazy to go. 'Why do you want to talk with *them*?' they asked me."

Selwa's struggles are bound up with her family. "I have a teenage son called Simon. During the Intifada, he was attacked by Israeli soldiers. So we sent him to the United States to finish his studies. But he has so many emotional problems. He's been there five years and he's only finished one year of his studies. He has terrible nightmares. And this has really affected my family. My husband is stressed and spends all his time in the coffee shop…"

So had the conference helped Selwa? She smiled, "I am not afraid to visit an Israeli woman any more. She is no longer my enemy. I have spoken to my neighbours – the ones who laughed at me for attending the conference. They see the good in it now. And I think in this way, there will be progress for the future."

But doubt clouded her eyes and Selwa suddenly turned to me, "Can this conference really bring results?" The tables were turned, and I saw the naked longing in their eyes. The weariness of hostilities. "There has been so much suffering – on both sides," she said. I fumbled with inadequate words. What could I say? I had never been in their position. I was saved by Hanan.

"We women have the power to change things. Look at the Bible! There are many examples of women who did just that!"

We all smiled, and I gathered up my equipment to leave, with a new sense of optimism in my heart.

Open Doors International Vision Statement

We believe that all doors are open and that God enables his body to go into all the world and preach the Gospel. We therefore define our ministry as follows:

- To strengthen the body of Christ living under restriction or persecution by providing and delivering Bibles, materials, training and other helps, and encouraging it to become involved in world evangelism.

- To train and encourage the body of Christ in threatened or unstable areas, to prepare believers to face persecution and suffering, and to equip them to maintain a witness to the Gospel of Christ.

- To motivate, mobilise, and educate the Church in the free world to identify with and become more involved in assisting the Suffering Church, believing that when *"one members suffers, all the members suffer with it"* (1 Corinthians 12:26 NKJV).

How you and your church can make a difference

Prayer – the believers in persecuted lands live in a fierce spiritual battlefield. They need focused, intercessory prayer. Open Doors prayer magazines and newsletters provide you with daily prayer items to enable you to pray for these brothers and sisters and stand beside them in their struggle.

Bible Couriers – for decades, Open Doors has been helping believers carry Bibles and Bible study aids into the areas of greatest persecution. God uses ordinary people to take his Word to people living where faith costs the most. You can be one of them.

Adult and Children's Bibles – many persecuted believers have been beaten and imprisoned for their faith, yet don't have a Bible of their own. The young people in persecuted lands are special targets for false teaching and government control. Leaders know they must have control of the minds of the youth if they are to stop the spread of Christianity. Open Doors is providing the Church with special adult and children's Bibles that present the truth through words and pictures. Your generous gifts make this possible.

Leadership Training for Church Growth and Evangelism – most church leaders in persecuted lands have never had any formal training. Bible Schools either don't exist or have been destroyed. Open Doors works to fill this vacuum in these lands with Bible-based training tailored to the needs and culture of each area.

Your faith can equip and encourage the future leaders of our fellow believers who suffer for their faith.

For more information, write to:

Open Doors
PO Box 53
Seaforth
NSW 2092
AUSTRALIA

Missao Portas Abertas
CP 45371
Vila Mariana
CEP 04010-970
São Paulo
BRAZIL

Open Doors
PO Box 597
Streetsville, ONT
L5M 2C1
CANADA

Portes Ouvertes
BP 141
67833 TANNERIES
Cédex
FRANCE

Porte Aperte
CP 45
37063 Isola della Scala
Verona
ITALY

Open Doors
Hyerim Presbyterian
   Church
Street No 403
Sungne 3-dong
Kangdong-gu #134-033
Seoul
KOREA

Open Doors
PO Box 47
3850 AA Ermelo
THE NETHERLANDS

Open Doors
PO Box 27-630
Mt Roskill
Auckland 1030
NEW ZEALAND

Åpne Dorer
PO Box 4698 Grim
4673 Kristiansand
NORWAY

Open Doors
PO Box 1573-1155
QCCPO Main
1100 Quezon City
PHILIPPINES

Open Doors
1 Sophia Road
#06-11 Peace Centre
SINGAPORE 228149

Open Doors
Box 990099
Kibler Park 2053
Johannesburg
SOUTH AFRICA

Portes Ouvertes
Case Postale 267
CH-1008 Prilly
Lausanne
SWITZERLAND

Open Doors
PO Box 6
Witney
Oxon OX8 7SP
UNITED KINGDOM

Open Doors
PO Box 27001
Santa Ana
CA 92799
USA

You can visit the Open Doors website on www.od org